YOUR KNOWLEDGE HAS VALUE

- We will publish your bachelor's and master's thesis, essays and papers

- Your own eBook and book - sold worldwide in all relevant shops

- Earn money with each sale

Upload your text at www.GRIN.com and publish for free

Felix Wiebrecht

Is the European Union a peculiar political system or a very developed international organization?

GRIN Verlag

Bibliografische Information der Deutschen Nationalbibliothek:

Die Deutsche Bibliothek verzeichnet diese Publikation in der Deutschen National-
bibliografie; detaillierte bibliografische Daten sind im Internet über http://dnb.d-
nb.de/ abrufbar.

Dieses Werk sowie alle darin enthaltenen einzelnen Beiträge und Abbildungen
sind urheberrechtlich geschützt. Jede Verwertung, die nicht ausdrücklich vom
Urheberrechtsschutz zugelassen ist, bedarf der vorherigen Zustimmung des Verla-
ges. Das gilt insbesondere für Vervielfältigungen, Bearbeitungen, Übersetzungen,
Mikroverfilmungen, Auswertungen durch Datenbanken und für die Einspeicherung
und Verarbeitung in elektronische Systeme. Alle Rechte, auch die des auszugsweisen
Nachdrucks, der fotomechanischen Wiedergabe (einschließlich Mikrokopie) sowie
der Auswertung durch Datenbanken oder ähnliche Einrichtungen, vorbehalten.

Imprint:

Copyright © 2013 GRIN Verlag GmbH
Druck und Bindung: Books on Demand GmbH, Norderstedt Germany
ISBN: 978-3-656-47182-0

This book at GRIN:

http://www.grin.com/en/e-book/215582/is-the-european-union-a-peculiar-political-
system-or-a-very-developed-international

GRIN - Your knowledge has value

Der GRIN Verlag publiziert seit 1998 wissenschaftliche Arbeiten von Studenten, Hochschullehrern und anderen Akademikern als eBook und gedrucktes Buch. Die Verlagswebsite www.grin.com ist die ideale Plattform zur Veröffentlichung von Hausarbeiten, Abschlussarbeiten, wissenschaftlichen Aufsätzen, Dissertationen und Fachbüchern.

Visit us on the internet:

http://www.grin.com/

http://www.facebook.com/grincom

http://www.twitter.com/grin_com

Is the European Union a peculiar political system or a very developed political system?

Felix Wiebrecht
PI1515: Introduction to Political Science

The EU nowadays is a very powerful political actor and has a very big influence, not only in

Europe, but also in the rest of the world. Starting from a community for joint coal and steel

administration it developed further and further. Today there is a discussion among scholars about

the type of political actor the EU constitutes. Is it an international organization, a political system, a

supranational state or something completely new and incomparable. This paper wants to prove that

the European Union is not an international organization, despite having some of the appropriate

characteristics, but rather a political system. In order to achieve that it will try to define the terms

'political system' and 'international organization' and then evaluate if the characteristics of those

match with the European Union as a political actor.

The first term this paper would like to analyse is the expression 'international organization'.

Following Rittberger and Zangl (2006) there are several characteristics of such institutions. First of

all it is often said that through these establishments states often try to achieve aims that are in the

national interest but not necessarily beneficial for all states and decisions which are made "primarily

reflect the interests of the most powerful member states" (Rittberger and Zangl, 2006:6) Moreover

international organizations are defined as "permanent institutions of conference diplomacy in which

states may exchange information, condemn or justify certain actions and coordinate their national

political strategies." (Rittberger and Zangl, 2006:6) Despite emphasizing the member states and

their national interests in the first two characteristics, international organizations are also marked by

1

pooled or delegated sovereignty coming from the member states so that these institutions become "corporate actors" (Rittberger and Zangl, 2006:6) themselves. Furthermore the decisions are made by several states and "the crucial point here is that without the relevant organization decisions would not have been made in the same way." (Rittberger and Zangl, 2006:6) However, the authors distinguish between "international regimes" and "international organizations", saying that former only focus on one specific area of interest, for instance like the World Health Organisation which is concerned about health issues. Unlike those 'international regimes' 'international organizations' cover a lot more topics than only one area of interest.

According to this distinction the European Union is clearly an international organization as it is involved in different areas of topics, that becomes clear if we look for instance at the three pillars of the European Union. Already the first comprises different areas of politics as part of the EU's competences, varying from consumer protection to asylum policy.

Also, the European Union meets the criteria of pooled and delegated legislation. Unlike a federalist system, where competences are determined between different institutions, the member states decided to give some power to an institution that is supranational, that means beyond the borders of a nation. This means the EU can only be as powerful as the member states decide the European Union should be because they are the basis for the EU's power. In fact, it is hard to imagine that laws would exist that are valid everywhere in Europe without the European Union.

Additionally it is also true that the European Union is an "instrument with which states pursue their own interest best as they can" (Rittberger and Zangl, 2006:6) One can evaluate that when looking at the different institutions of the EU. The various member states have got two institutions in which they can directly express their intentions. These are the Council of Ministers and the European Council, both of them are intergovernmental institutions and are based on the national interests. One could argue that the decisions made in the last months and years regarding the European Financial Crisis are in favour of the more powerful countries, especially Germany who profits disproportionate high from the undervalued Euro and so it can continue to export its products for lower prices, but are not willing to change their policy so that other European countries would not be disadvantaged.

Also the permanent exchange of information is given in the European Union through the various institutions, like the Commission, the Council of Ministers or the European Parliament in which continuous debates are taking place and through a law-making process that requires different institution' approvals

In contrast stands the term 'political system' which comprises much more aspects. Despite the fact that their works are now nearly 60 years old the aspects that Almond (1956) and Easton (1957) found to define the term, have survived. They found four main characteristics of political systems to which "a stable and clearly defined set of institutions for collective decision-making and a set of rules governing relations between and within these institutions" (Hix, 2005:2) belongs. Moreover they say that "citizens and social groups seek to realize their political desires through the political system" (Hix, 2005:2) which could be done directly or through the means of organisations and political parties. Furthermore decisions being made influence "the distribution of economic resources and the allocation of social and political values across the whole system" (Hix, 2005:2) notably. Finally they say that there is permanent "interaction between these political outputs, new demands on the system, new decisions and so on." (Hix, 2005:2) That means that there is constantly feedback from both, the governing and the governed to the other.

It is not arguable that the European Union has a set of institutions for the joint decision-making process. This set comprises the Commission, the Council of Ministers, the European Council and the European Parliament. Moreover, rules governing and defining the relation between the institutions and within them are mostly written down in the 'Treaty on Functioning of European Union' (TFEU).

Also the second characteristic seems to match with the European Union, because there is a huge variety of people and institutions making demands to the system of the EU, which are "ranging from individual corporations and business associations to trade unions, environment and consumer

3

groups and political parties." (Hix, 2005:3) The most powerful groups are hereby the national governments and those political parties, the government consists of. However, every citizen of an EU member-state can start a petition.

In addition to that, also the European Union's decisions "are highly significant and felt throughout the EU." (Hix, 2005:3) This fact is caused by different aspects to which the feature belongs that the EU covers a wide variety of policies, ranging from market regulation to education and culture, but also the fact that more pieces of legislation pass through the EU institutions every year than in most other democratic systems. Hereby it is also important to stress that EU law overrules national laws and that "EU regulatory and monetary policies have a powerful indirect impact on the distribution of power and resources between individuals, groups and nations in Europe." (Hix, 2005:3)

Furthermore also the continuous feedback applies to the system of the European Union, for instance visible at the example of the planned privatisation of water supply which was immediately opposed by a petition against this plan.

In conclusion of this confrontation it is possible to say that the European Union matches the criteria of being an international organization as well as the characteristics of political systems. However, although the EU's characteristics are in accordance to those like other international organization such like the World Trade Organisation or the International Labour Organisation it is arguable if the EU is on the same level as those ones regarding their influence, significance, opportunities to participate and autonomy and that is why one could bring forward the argument that the European Union indeed matches the features of international organizations but it even reaches further than that. The main aspect to look at here is that the European Union "functions like a state, i.e. a sovereign polity endowed with the autonomy and legitimacy necessary to impose its decisions on a defined population and territory" (Martinelli, 2007:8) The question that comes up is whether the European Union should be looked at rather as a supranational state than an organization.

There are arguments speaking in favour of considering the EU as a state, for instance as Lelieveldt Princen point out: " Just like national political systems the EU makes binding decisions in a way that is very similar to how national democratic systems operate. Its institutions perform legislative, executive and judicial tasks and are structured in a quite similar fashion to that of national political systems." (2011:44) Furthermore the EU covers a broad range of policy areas, there is a fairly elected body, the EU uses the qualified majority voting system on many issues and EU law is supreme over national law. However, one should consider the European Union neither as a state nor as a nation-state because it lacks some essential characteristics of states, to which missing taxes, a missing police force and a missing army belong, in other words "what Max Weber distinguished as the most significant features of the sovereignty of a modern state: monopoly over legitimized violence, fiscal authority, and effective law enforcement institutions." (Martinelli, 2007:8) Moreover the EU does not possess "what German lawyers call 'Kompetenz-Kompetenz': the competence to define its own competences." (Lelieveldt and Princen, 2011:294)

Conclusive looking at the European Union this paper proofed that this institution is not an international organization, although it meets the criteria of such, because the EU's competence is much more far-reaching than any other international organization's competence. However, one cannot look at the European Union as a state since it is lacking the state's power of monopolised legitimized violence.

Bibliography:

Almond, G., 1956. Comparative Political Systems. *The Journal of Politic*, [e-journal] 18(3).
Available through: JSTOR database <http://web.unair.ac.id/admin/file/f_23123_CP_Almond.pdf>

Easton, D., 1957. An Approach to the Analysis of Political Systems. *World Politics,* [e-journal] 9(3).
Available through: JSTOR database
<http://www.jstor.org/stable/pdfplus/2008920.pdfacceptTC=true>

Hix, S. *The Political System of the European Union* 2nd edt. 2005 New York: Palgrave Macmillan

Lelieveldt, H. and Princen, S. *The Politics of The European Union.* 2011 Cambridge: Cambridge
University Press

Martinelli, A., 2007. *The Political Democracies of the United States and the European Union* [pdf]
Available at: <http://www.socpol.unimi.it/papers/2006-12-12_Martinelli%20Alberto.pdf>
[Accessed 15 April 2013].

Rittberger, V. and Zangl, B., 2006. *International Organization – Polity, Politics and Policies.* New
York: Palgrave Macmillan